# WILDFLOWERS
## of the Mountain Southwest

D0250025

Meg Quinn

Rio Nuevo Publishers

Tucson, Arizona

## Vista Grande
## Public Library
## T 114005

*The author wishes to thank Phil Jenkins of the University of Arizona
Herbarium and Anita Harlan of the University of Arizona Ecology
and Evolutionary Ecology Department for reviewing the manuscript.
Thanks also to the talented photographers—Dave Bertelsen, Ron
Coleman, Jim Honcoop, George H. H. Huey, Jon Mark Stewart, and
Mills Tandy—who contributed their stunning images to this guide.*

Rio Nuevo Publishers
An imprint of Treasure Chest Books
P.O. Box 5250
Tucson, AZ 85703-0250

© 2003 Meg Quinn
All Rights Reserved

No part of this publication may be reproduced, stored, or introduced
into a retrieval system, or likewise copied in any form without the
prior written permission of the publisher, excepting quotes for review
or citation.

Photographs
© David Bertelsen: pages 27, 41, 53, 65 (top), 70, 78
© Ronald Coleman: pages 29, 32, 33, 36, 37, 39, 42, 43
© Jim Honcoop: pages 1, 6, 7, 31, 47, 48, 49 (top), 51, 58 (top), 80
(bottom), 81
© George H. H. Huey: front cover
© Meg Quinn: pages 3, 9, 10, 11, 12, 13, 14, 15, 17, 19, 20, 21, 26, 45, 46,
52 (top), 64, 66, 67, 69, 72 (bottom), 73, 76, 77, 80 (top), 85
© Jon Mark Stewart: pages 16, 18, 22, 23, 24, 25, 28, 30, 34, 35, 38, 40,
44, 50, 52 (bottom), 54, 55, 56, 57, 60, 61, 62, 63, 71, 72 (top), 75
© Mills Tandy: title page, pages 5, 8, 49 (bottom), 58 (middle, bottom), 59,
65 (bottom), 68, 74, 82
Map (page 2) and flower illustrations (page 4) © Paul Mirocha

Library of Congress Cataloging-in-Publication Data

Quinn, Meg.
    Wildflowers of the Mountain Southwest / Meg Quinn.
        p. cm.
    ISBN 1-887896-36-8 (pbk.)
1. Wild flowers—Southwest, New—Identification. 2. Mountain plants—
Southwest, New—Identification. 3. Wild flowers—Southwest, New—
Pictorial works. 4. Mountain plants—Southwest, New—Pictorial works.
I. Title.
    QK142.Q56 2003
    582.13'0979—dc21                          2003007208

Printed in Korea

10   9   8   7   6   5   4   3   2   1

# Introduction

WITHDRAWN

In the American Southwest, the massive Rocky Mountain chain tapers down into a number of smaller ranges at its southern tip. Also in this region, the Sierra Madre Occidental—a large, geologically distinct range extending south well into northern Mexico—reaches up into the Southwestern United States. This commingling of ecosystems contributes to the richness and  diversity of the flora of the Southwest region, particularly along the US border states. These borderland ranges are referred to as "sky islands," due to their separation from one another by "seas" of desert scrub and grasslands. In these mountains, we find some unique species of wildfowers that do not occur anywhere else in the US.

Many Southwest mountain peaks reach well over 9,000 feet and can be as much as 20 degrees cooler than the surrounding desert on a hot summer day. For each 1,000 foot climb in elevation, the temperature will drop an average of three degrees Fahrenheit. From a number of easily accessible roads, one can easily journey to the top of a high peak in just a few hours and, in so doing, pass through several biotic communities, or groupings of plants and animals that occur together. These can be recognized as distinct belts of vegetation that grade into one another and usually include desert scrub, grassland, chaparral, oak woodland, pine-oak woodland, pine, mixed conifer, and spruce-fir forests.

For wildflower enthusiasts, these montane peaks become a floral paradise in summer. In response to warm temperatures and summer rains, annual and perennial wildflowers rapidly grow and blossom, some dotting forest trails, others creating colorful displays "en masse" in mountain meadows. In observing mountain wildflowers, one begins to notice their habitat preferences. Some species occur only in sunny meadows, while others require shade, very wet conditions along streams, or rocky soils. One quickly learns that the more varied the types of habitats visited, the greater the number of species likely to be encountered. Peak flowering for mountain wildflowers will vary from mid-summer to early fall, depending on latitude, elevation, and climatic conditions.

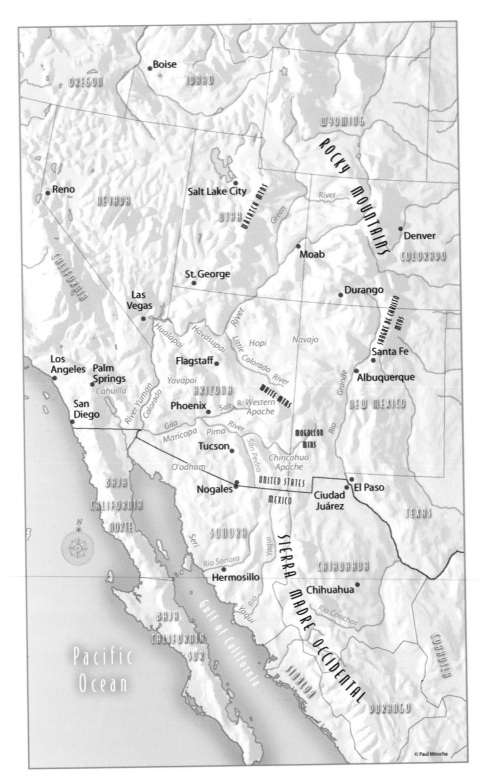

## About This Book

This guide is designed for anyone with an interest in mountain wildflowers. Plants described in the text include a sampling of annuals and perennials occurring in Southwestern mountains at elevations of 7,000 feet to about 10,000 feet. In general this will include the biotic communities of pine forest, mixed conifer forest, and spruce-fir forest. For our purposes the term "Southwest" includes Arizona, New Mexico, Colorado, Utah, and northern Mexico. However, many of the species shown also occur in the montane regions of neighboring states, including California and Texas. Flowers are arranged by color, and within each color category they are ordered alphabetically by scientific name. Botanical terms used in the text are defined in the glossary at the back of the book.

Traditional and modern-day uses of some plants have been noted, but only as a point of interest. Many plants are extremely toxic to humans, and readers should not attempt to use them as a food or medicine unless thoroughly trained in plant identification and proper processing techniques.

## Plant Names

Common, scientific, and family names appear for each wildflower. Common names vary considerably in different locales and can create confusion for anyone attempting to identify wildflowers. A plant may have several common names, and one

common name may be applied to multiple plant species that are similar in appearance. Scientific names are somewhat more reliable, although these names are occasionally changed and updated by botanists. A two-word, Latin scientific name is assigned to each species and consists of a genus and species name, as in *Dugaldia hoopesii*. The genus name is given to a number of species with shared characteristics. The family is a broader classification above that of genus and is also given a common and scientific name, such as sunflower family (Asteraceae). Terms such as variety (var.) and subspecies (ssp.) are occasionally used and mean about the same thing. Both refer to geographic populations that are genetically distinct but not enough to be named as a new species. This guide attempts to use the most widely accepted common names and currently updated scientific names. Synonyms for scientific names that have been recently changed appear in the index.

# Flower Structures

Basic flower structure generally consists of four parts. The outer part, usually greenish, is the calyx and is made up of sepals. Within the calyx lies the often colorful corolla, composed of petals. Inside the petals and often attached to the corolla are the stamens or "male" part of the flower. Each stamen consists of a filament with a pollen-bearing anther at the tip. In the center of the flower lies at least one pistil, the "female" part of the flower. Its swollen base, or ovary, contains ovules that will develop into seeds. Above the ovary sits the style, a slender stalk, topped by a stigma designed to receive pollen. Pollen is typically either wind-borne or transported by a pollinator to the stigma of a flower. The pollen produces the sperm that fertilize the ovules within the ovary. After fertilization, the ovary matures into a dry or fleshy fruit containing the seeds.

Many of the plants shown in this guide are members of the sunflower family (Asteraceae) and deserve special mention due to the unique structure and arrangement of their flowers. Asters, dandelions, and daisies are all examples of plants in the sunflower family, producing

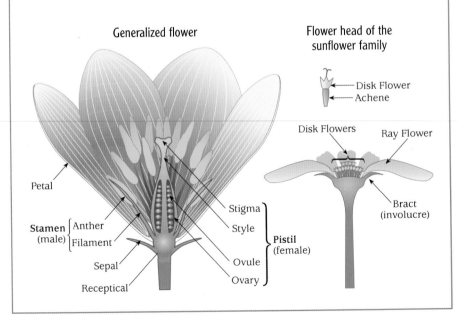

Generalized flower

Flower head of the sunflower family

Disk Flower
Achene

Disk Flowers
Ray Flower

Petal

Stamen { Anther
(male) { Filament

Sepal

Receptical

Stigma
Style
Ovule
Ovary
} Pistil (female)

Bract (involucre)

flower heads that may appear to be single flowers. Actually, these heads consist of numerous small tubular "disk" flowers, packed together in the center and surrounded by strap-shaped "ray" flowers. Depending on the species, a flower head can be all rays, all disk, or a combination of the two. The calyx is absent or reduced to bristles, scales, or hairs. At the base of the flower head lie greenish, leaf-like bracts. ❀

# Monk's Hood

## Aconitum columbianum

**Buttercup family (Ranunculaceae)**

Monk's hood, a tuberous perennial with bluish-purple flowers, can be found along mountain streams, in shady forests, or in open meadows with abundant moisture. A close examination of the flowers reveals 5 petal-like sepals with a large helmet-shaped sepal forming a hood. Two rounded sepals lie on the sides of the flower and 2 along the base. The actual petals are small and concealed beneath the hood. Flowering stems can be up to 6 feet tall, bearing palmately lobed leaves with jagged margins. All parts of the plant are extremely poisonous, containing aconite and other alkaloids. European monk's hood, *A. napellus,* although potentially lethal, has been used to treat a variety of ailments. The alkaloid-free roots of *A. carmichaelii* are used in Chinese herbal medicine.

**Elevation:** 5,000 to 9,500 feet
**Range:** Canada to California, Arizona, and New Mexico

# Harebells, Bluebells

## Campanula rotundifolia

**Bellflower family (Campanulaceae)**

Delicate lavender-blue, sometimes pink, harebells hang on slender stalks 1 to 2 feet in height. The ¾-inch-long flowers are distinctly bell-shaped, with several blossoms dangling on each stem. Plants are perennial with milky sap, woody rhizomes, and linear- to lance-shaped leaves alternating on the stems. The name rotundifolia refers to the rounded basal leaves. Harebells are extremely common in high meadows and on rocky slopes and are widespread in the mountains of North America and Eurasia. Navajos rubbed crushed harebell leaves on their bodies for protection from injury while hunting. This plant should not be confused with the unrelated *Mertensia* species that have more cylindrical blossoms and are called bluebells or chiming bells.

**Elevation:** 8,000 to 12,000 feet
**Range:** throughout western North America and Eurasia

# Star-Thistle

## Centaurea rothrockii

### Sunflower family (Asteraceae)

The showy, 4-inch-wide flower heads of star-thistle are a dazzling sight to behold along streams, on mountain slopes, and in forest clearings. Heads consist entirely of creamy-yellow disk flowers, with an outer ring of deep rose-pink to purple flowers. The wide heads make an ideal "landing platform" for the multitude of butterflies and insects attracted to the flowers and serving as its pollinators. Plants grow to about 3 feet in height and bear toothless, lance-shaped leaves. The similar and more widespread *C. americana* also occurs in the Southwest and has been commonly cultivated under the name of American basketflower. Several exotic *Centaurea* species known as "knapweed" have spiny-toothed bracts and are considered noxious weeds in some Western states.

**Elevation:** 6,000 to 8,000 feet
**Range:** southwestern New Mexico, southeastern Arizona to Oaxaca, Mexico

# Dayflower

## Commelina dianthifolia

**Spiderwort family (Commeliniaceae)**

Rich, royal-blue flowers with a large, translucent bract beneath each blossom make this plant easy to recognize along shaded mountain trails. Each ¾-inch-wide, 3-petaled flower blooms for just one day, hence the common name of dayflower. Leaves are alternately arranged on thick stems, with the leaf bases clasping the stems. Dayflower grows to a foot or more in height and is commonly found in pine and mixed conifer forests. Navajos gave an infusion of the plant to their livestock as an aphrodisiac. The related spiderwort, *Tradescantia pinetorum,* occurs in a similar range and elevation but lacks the distinctive bract beneath the flowers, which are violet or purple in color.

**Elevation:** 3,500 to 9,500 feet
**Range:** southwestern US and throughout Mexico

# Larkspur

## Delphinium andesicola

**Buttercup family (Ranunculaceae)**

A perennial herb commonly forming dense stands in moist, open meadows, larkspur will grow to 4 feet in height under good conditions. The 1-inch-long flowers consist of 5 petals and 5 sepals, with the uppermost sepal forming a long, nectar-rich spur. Leaves are deeply cut into segments with jagged margins and occur primarily at the base of the plant. Hummingbirds zealously feed on the flowers and serve as pollinators. *Delphinium* species contain delphine and other toxic alkaloids and are highly poisonous to cattle. Many species occur throughout North America and are cultivated for their showy blooms. *D. andesicola* reaches its northern limit in the border ranges of southeastern Arizona. Subalpine larkspur, *D. barbeyi,* is found from Wyoming to Arizona and New Mexico.

**Elevation:** 5,000 to 9,500 feet
**Range:** border ranges of southeastern Arizona

# Western Fringed Gentian

## Gentianopsis macrantha

**Gentian family (Gentianaceae)**

Found in moist, sunny meadows and bogs throughout the West, western fringed gentian is a handsome annual wildflower that bears showy, 1- to 2-inch-long, deep-blue to purple flowers, each with 4 ornately fringed petals and 4 fused sepals. Narrow, lance-shaped leaves oppose each other on the stems. Western fringed gentian grows 1 to 2 feet in height and is found on moist slopes and in wet meadows at elevations above 8,000 feet throughout the West. The roots have been used as a digestive stimulant. The Rocky Mountain race of this wide-ranging species was known as *G. thermalis* but is now considered a synonym of *G. macrantha*.

**Elevation:** 8,000 to 11,000 feet
**Range:** Canada south to Arizona and New Mexico

# Western Pink Vervain

## Glandularia bipinnatifida

**Verbena family (Verbenaceae)**

Brilliant pink to purple clusters of ½-inch-wide flowers adorn the stem tips of western pink vervain and are frequented by numerous bees and butterflies. The leaves are dark green and pinnately divided with sunken veins. Plants grow to a height of 10 to 16 inches and form colorful low mounds in mountain meadows and open coniferous forests. Formerly known as *Verbena,* the genus *Glandularia* is widespread in North America, and a variety of species have been used by Native Americans and modern herbalists to treat colds, coughs, fevers, and stomach cramps. Members of the genus are widely cultivated in gardens for their showy blossoms.

**Elevation:** 5,000 to 10,000 feet
**Range:** Arizona, New Mexico, Texas, Oklahoma, and northern Mexico

# Mock Pennyroyal

## Hedeoma hyssopifolia

**Mint family (Lamiaceae)**

Delicate, ½-inch-long, lavender flowers with white throats occur in pairs along the multiple stems of this 1- to 2-foot-tall perennial herb. The narrow, pointed, aromatic, opposing leaves lack teeth on the margins. Mock pennyroyal is found on open hillsides, in canyons, and in shady pine and mixed-conifer forests. It has been used as a medicinal treatment for coughs and digestive disorders, and leaves can be rubbed on the body as an effective insect repellent. In the US, the genus *Hedeoma* is limited primarily to the Southwest and Texas regions. It also occurs in parts of Mexico and South America.

**Elevation:** 5,000 to 9,500 feet
**Range:** Arizona, New Mexico, and northern Mexico

# Rocky Mountain Iris, Blue Flag

## Iris missouriensis

**Iris family (Iridaceae)**

Found throughout the Western states in moist meadows and along stream banks, Rocky Mountain iris produces showy bluish-purple flowers similar to those of its garden relatives. Look for 3 upright petals and 3 downward-curving petal-like sepals with yellow streaks and purple veins. The flowers can be 3 to 4 inches wide and sit atop a leafless stalk up to 3 feet tall. Leaves are flattened and sword-like, 8 to 20 inches tall, with parallel veins. After flowering, fruits develop into erect capsules with 3 sections and many seeds. Native Americans used a tea of the roots for stomach disorders and kidney and bladder problems, and they made poultices for sores, bruises, aches, and pains. The plant contains toxins that can be harmful to humans and livestock when eaten.

**Elevation:** 6,000 to 9,000 feet
**Range:** throughout western North America

# Lupine

## Lupinus blumeri

**Pea family (Fabaceae)**

A widespread genus throughout western North America, lupines, or members of the genus *Lupinus,* are easy to recognize with their characteristic palmate leaves and pea-like flowers arranged on a spike-like flowering stem. *L. blumeri* is a perennial species endemic to southeastern Arizona, with a range that overlaps with the more widespread *L. palmeri.* Although similar in appearance, *L. blumeri* has larger flowers. Seedpods of lupine will suddenly split open when mature and eject seeds away from the mother plant. Many lupines are considered desirable landscape plants and are commonly cultivated in gardens. Annual desert species form spectacular carpets of flowers in a good wildflower year.

**Elevation:** 6,000 to 9,000 feet
**Range:** border ranges of southeastern Arizona

# Field Mint

## Mentha arvensis

**Mint family (Lamiaceae)**

Field mint is an aromatic perennial with opposing leaves, square stems, and creeping rhizomes. Pale pink to lavender flowers occur in crowded clusters around the upper leaf axils. The tapered, dark green leaves are up to 3 inches long, noticeably toothed, and broadly lance-shaped. Field mint requires moist soils and is especially abundant along streams. Native Americans have used field mint to treat colds, flu, sore throat, gas, nausea, and stomach disorders. Modern herbalists use related *Mentha* species in similar ways, particularly as a soothing tonic for the digestive system. European pennyroyal, *M. pulegium,* has been used as an insect repellent to deter fleas, mites, and ticks from human skin and as a flea repellent for dogs. Fresh leaves were often strewn in dwellings to repel bedbugs and other insects.

**Elevation:** 5,000 to 9,500 feet
**Range:** widespread throughout North America and around the globe

# Franciscan Bluebells, Chiming Bells

## Mertensia franciscana

**Borage family (Boraginaceae)**

A common feature of alpine and subalpine forests and meadows throughout the West, Franciscan bluebells are noted for the hanging clusters of cylindrical dark blue to pale blue flowers. Each flower is 5-lobed, to ⅝ inch long, with hairy sepal margins. Leaves are lance-shaped and alternate along the stems. Plants vary from 1 to 3 feet in height, depending on conditions. Members of the genus *Mertensia* are sometimes called lungworts, referring to a European species thought to be a remedy for lung disease. *M. virginica* has been documented as a treatment for whooping cough and tuberculosis by the Cherokee.

**Elevation:** 7,000 to 10,000 feet
**Range:** western Colorado and Utah to New Mexico and Arizona

# Bee-Balm, Horsemint

## Monarda austromontana

**Mint family (Lamiaceae)**

The lavender-purple flowers of this particular species of bee-balm occur in crowded clusters along the stems and tips of the plants, which grow to about a foot in height. Lance-shaped leaves are in an opposite arrangement on the square stems. Bee-balm is a perennial with extremely aromatic foliage. It is sometimes called Mexican oregano and has been used as a seasoning and a medicine. *Monarda* species contain tymol, an antiseptic compound used in mouthwash. Several species of *Monarda* have

been traditionally used by Native Americans to treat digestive problems and as a perfume for both people and horses.

**Elevation**: 4,000 to 8,500 feet
**Range**: southwestern New Mexico, Arizona, and northern Mexico

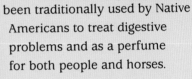

# Wandloom Penstemon

## Penstemon virgatus

**Figwort family (Scrophulariaceae)**

Wandloom penstemon flowers are pale violet with deep-purple lines in the throat to guide bee pollinators to nectar at the base of the corolla. The slightly inflated blossoms are funnel-shaped, with two flared lobes on the upper corolla and three below. The tongue-like sterile stamen lacks the hairs found in other species. Leaves are dark green, narrow, and linear, and the entire plant in full bloom can be up to 2½ feet tall but is usually much shorter. It is commonly found in pine forests and mountain meadows. Members of the large genus *Penstemon* are generally short-lived perennials and produce just a basal rosette of leaves in the first year. The following year flowering stems shoot up, often creating a spectacular display. Penstemons are extremely popular garden plants, and most are easily grown from seed. More than 35 species of *Penstemon* are native to Arizona.

**Elevation:** 5,000 to 11,000 feet
**Range:** New Mexico and Arizona

# Jacob's Ladder

## Polemonium foliosissimum

**Phlox family (Polemoniaceae)**

Jacob's ladder is an herbaceous perennial that grows to a height of about 3 feet and favors moist soils in shady forests, along mountain streams, and in wet meadows. Leaves resemble long ladders, giving the plant its common name. The 1-inch-wide flowers occur in clusters at the stem tips, typically pale to medium blue but sometimes white or purple. Pinnate leaves with simple, lance-like leaflets alternate along the stems. A related species known as sky pilot, *P. viscosum,* bears clusters of trumpet-shaped violet-blue blossoms, and stems and leaves covered with sticky glandular hairs.

**Elevation:** 8,000 to 9,000 feet
**Range:** Colorado, Utah, New Mexico, and Arizona

# Rusby Primrose

## Primula rusbyi

**Primrose family (Primulaceae)**

The rich, magenta flowers of Rusby primrose are produced in loose clusters on flower stalks up to 10 inches in height. Individual blooms are comprised of 5 spreading lobes joined into a narrow tube with yellow markings at the throat. Flowers bloom within 1 to 2 weeks following the first summer rains and are typically found on rocky ledges above 7,500 feet. Rusby primrose is restricted in the US to southeastern Arizona and New Mexico. A similar and more widely distributed species, Parry primrose, *P. parryi,* occurs above 10,000 feet, is a larger plant, and bears flowers having the distinct odor of carrion, which are likely pollinated by flies drawn to the disagreeable odor.

**Elevation:** 7,500 to 10,000 feet
**Range:** New Mexico, southeastern Arizona, and Mexico

# Heal All

## Prunella vulgaris

**Mint family (Lamiaceae)**

A low-growing perennial reaching 3 to 12 inches in height, heal all bears dark purple to lavender 2-lipped flowers clustered on a stout oblong spike. Leaves are opposing on slender, square stems. Heal all is well-known among herbalists and Native Americans for its curative properties. It has been used for healing wounds, sore throat, gum disease, fevers, colds, coughs, stomach ailments, and heart problems. Recent studies have shown that plant extracts of heal all demonstrate antibacterial and antioxidant effects, as well as blood-pressure-lowering properties. Heal all has naturalized throughout the cooler parts of North America in a variety of habitats including moist meadows, roadsides, and stream banks.

**Elevation:** 5,000 to 9,000 feet
**Range:** throughout North America and Europe

# American Vetch

## Vicia americana var. linearis

**Pea family (Fabaceae)**

One of many types of "pea vines" commonly encountered in Southwest mountains, American vetch grows to 2 to 4 feet in height and bears pinnate leaves and stems with pronounced tendrils. Attractive lavender to purple pea flowers emerge in loose clusters from the axils of the leaves. Look for the inconspicuous toothed stipules (leaf-like appendages) at the base of each leaf stalk. Although typical *V. americana* has oval-shaped leaflets, *Vicia americana* var. *linearis* bears distinctly narrow leaflets. Fruits consist of 1-inch-long, flat, hairless pods. American vetch prefers clearings and open sites in pine and mixed conifer forests. Some *Vicia* species bear a close resemblance to members of the genus *Lathyrus.* They can be distinguished by looking closely at the arrangement of the hairs on the style tip. In *Vicia,* the hairs surround the tip, while in *Lathyrus,* they occur on the upper surface. Some vetches are considered highly poisonous and should not be consumed.

**Elevation:** 5,000 to 10,000 feet
**Range:** Canada to New Mexico, Arizona, California, and northeastern US

# Western Yarrow

## Achillea millefolium var. lanulosa

**Sunflower family (Asteraceae)**

Western yarrow is a perennial herb distinguished by its flat-topped clusters of small white to pinkish flowers and delicate, fernlike foliage. Both ray and disk flowers are present, though the rays are small and rounded. Stems are coated with cottony hairs, and the entire plant has a pungent odor. Western yarrow occurs in large patches in open meadows, clearings, and roadsides, growing to a height of 1 to 2 feet. Yarrow has a long history of use worldwide as a medicinal herb. It has been widely used as a remedy for a variety of respiratory ailments as well as a treatment for burns, sores, wounds, toothaches, insect bites, and gastrointestinal complaints.

**Elevation:** 8,500 to 11,000 feet
**Range:** widespread throughout North America

# Antelope Horns

## Asclepias asperula ssp. capricornu

**Milkweed family (Asclepiadaceae)**

A perennial that grows to about a foot in height, antelope horns bears 3-inch-wide clusters of greenish-yellow, fragrant flowers. Flowers have 5 sepals and 5 united petals with reflexed lobes, and stamens are united with the style to form a central column. Around the column are structures called "hoods" and within each lies a hornlike appendage. Pollen is contained in packets that attach to the legs of insects visiting the flowers. These packets then must slide into place on the column of the next flower in order for successful pollination to occur. Individual flowers are ½ inch wide and are followed by long green pods streaked with pink. As they mature, the pods burst open, releasing flat seeds attached to silky hairs, to be carried by the wind. Stems and leaves contain toxic milky sap and have been used by Navajos to induce vomiting during ceremonies.

**Elevation:** 3,000 to 9,000 feet
**Range:** Kansas and Arkansas to Texas, New Mexico, and Arizona

# Marsh Marigold, Elkslip

## Caltha leptosepala

**Buttercup family (Ranunculaceae)**

Marsh marigold has fleshy, rounded basal leaves and cup-shaped blossoms with numerous stamens in the center. The flowers do not have true petals—instead, there are 5 to 12 white, petal-like sepals. Each flower has several pistils that develop into erect follicles or pods. Usually only 2 to 12 inches in height, marsh marigold requires extremely moist habitats and is usually found along streams or in wet mountain meadows.

Although the leaves of *C. leptosepala* are poisonous when eaten raw, many Western tribes cooked and consumed the fleshy leaves and stems as a vegetable.

**Elevation:** 7,500 to 11,000 feet
**Range:** Alaska to Arizona and New Mexico

# Spotted Coralroot

## Corallorhiza maculata

**Orchid family (Orchidaceae)**

Spotted coralroot obtains nutrients from fungus in the soil and therefore produces minimal amounts of chlorophyll. As a result, it lacks true leaves, and the stems and flowers vary greatly in color, exhibiting shades of brown, pink, red, purple, and yellow. Flowers are about ¾ inch wide, with lightly veined and spotted sepals and petals. The conspicuous white lip is unevenly 3-lobed and usually dotted with reddish to purplish spots. Spotted coralroot is possibly the most common orchid in Arizona and New Mexico; however, one must seek it out during the blooming season, May through July. It is often found growing in the leaf litter of oaks,

conifers, and aspens, on rotting logs, and in moist environments along stream banks. Striped coralroot, also common in the Southwest, has prominent striping on all parts of the corolla and blooms from late April to early May.

**Elevation:** 6,900 to 10,000 feet
**Range:** Canada to Mexico

*Striped coralroot*

# Wood Strawberry

## Fragaria vesca ssp. bracteata

**Rose family (Rosaceae)**

Leaves bearing 3 prominently toothed leaflets make wood strawberry easy to spot when not in flower. The 1-inch-wide flowers are white with yellow centers and are followed by the tasty, ¾-inch, cone-shaped fruits. Plants propagate by runners that take root in the soil and by seeds distributed in droppings of animals that consume the fruits. Wood strawberry can be distinguished from other species by the tooth on the end of each leaflet, which projects beyond the adjacent teeth, and by seeds loosely attached to the surface of the fruit. Strawberry-leaf tea is high in vitamin C and has been used by herbalists as a medicine for fever, diarrhea, kidney problems, digestive disorders, and pollen allergies.

**Elevation:** 7,000 to 9,500 feet
**Range:** Canada to New Mexico, Arizona, and California

# Richardson's Geranium, White Geranium

## Geranium richardsonii

**Geranium family (Geraniaceae)**

**R**ichardson's geranium bears 1-inch-wide blossoms on the tips of stems that reach 1 to 3 feet in height. Prominent purple veins are visible on the petals and serve as nectar guides for pollinators. The palmately lobed leaves are divided into 3 to 7 segments with pointed tips, and hairs on the stems are tipped with red glands. Common and widespread in western North America, Richardson's geranium is encountered in moist, shady meadows and along streams, in aspen groves and in pine and mixed conifer forests. It is easily distinguished from *G. caespitosum,* a deep pink- to purple-flowered species. *G. wislizenii* bears white flowers noticeably smaller than *G. richardsonii's,* and it is limited in distribution to the mountains of southern Arizona, Texas, and northern Mexico.

**Elevation:** 6,500 to 11,500 feet
**Range:** Canada to New Mexico, Arizona, and southern California

# Rattlesnake Plantain

## Goodyera oblongifolia

**Orchid family (Orchidaceae)**

The foliage of rattlesnake plantain is unique and easily identifiable even when not in flower. Dark green, oblong leaves, each bearing a conspicuous white stripe along the midvein, form compact rosettes in shady oak or coniferous forests. Some plants also exhibit striking white veining on the leaves. These leafy rosettes will precede flowering by 3 years. Eventually, flowering stalks are produced and tiny white flowers emerge. Less than ½ inch long and ¼ inch wide, the bloom consists of greenish-white sepals and petals and a hood over the column and lip. Bees are the primary pollinators. Branching easily from a creeping root system, dense colonies of rattlesnake plantain will occur in some areas. Four species of *Goodyera* are known in North America and 2 in the

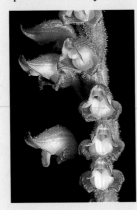

Southwest. *G. repens* is smaller in stature than *G. oblongifolia* and lacks the white striping on the leaves. *Goodyera* belongs to a group of orchids known collectively as the jewel orchids, often cultivated for their attractive foliage.

**Elevation:** 5,750 to 10,000 feet
**Range:** Alaska to northern Mexico

# Cow Parsnip

## Heracleum maximum

**Parsley family (Apiaceae)**

An unmistakable large, leafy plant, cow parsnip bears terminal clusters of creamy-white flowers in an umbel arrangement typical of the family. Each umbel may be up to 12 inches wide, and the plant itself ranges from 3 to 6 feet in height. In Alaska, plants can grow up to 10 feet tall. After flowering, small, round, flat fruits develop with noticeable dark lines. Leaves are often huge—up to 16 inches long with 3 large lobed and toothed leaflets. Cow parsnip is the largest member of the parsley family and is generally restricted to riparian habitats and moist meadows. Different parts of the plant have been used by Native Americans as a medicinal treatment for aching joints, wounds, sores, colds, stomach disorders, and headaches. Many tribes also ate the new young shoots as a raw vegetable in the spring. Just touching the plant, however, can cause dermatitis in some individuals. Be aware that certain members of the parsley family are deadly poisonous—do not ingest unless you are certain of the identity of the plant.

**Elevation:** 7,500 to 9,000 feet
**Range:** widespread throughout North America

# Arizona Pea

## Lathyrus arizonicus

**Pea family (Fabaceae)**

A white-flowered sprawling perennial, Arizona pea is widespread in coniferous forests throughout the Southwest. Flowers are ½ inch long and pea-like, 2 to 5 per cluster, with pinkish veins on the upper petal. Leaves are pinnately arranged, with 2 to 6 broadly linear leaflets. Tendrils are small and bristle-like, unlike other members of the genus *Lathyrus* that have prominent twining tendrils. The Chiricahua and Mescalero Apache have cooked and eaten ripe pods of the Arizona pea. The well-known garden sweet pea, *Lathyrus odoratus,* is a native of Sicily. Arizona pea resembles the vetches, *Vicia* species, but has larger flowers and fewer, larger leaflets.

**Elevation:** 8,000 to 11,000 feet

**Range:** from southeastern Utah to north-central Mexico

# Mountain Malaxis

## Malaxis soulei

**Orchid family (Orchidae)**

The genus *Malaxis* includes more than 300 species worldwide, with only 10 in North America and 4 found in Arizona and New Mexico. Mountain malaxis bears an inconspicuous flowering spike from a stem featuring only one relatively large, oval- to elliptic-shaped leaf. The diminutive flowers are best appreciated with a hand lens and vary from yellowish-green to dark green. Petals are green and threadlike; the lip is 3-lobed and notched at the top and bottom. Mountain malaxis is adapted to a variety of sites, from dry or wet meadows to open hillsides and rocky slopes, and is the most common and widespread member of the genus *Malaxis* in the Southwest. Related species are distinctly different and easy to distinguish. *M. porphyrea* has purple flowers that lean away from the stems. The greenish corollas of *M. corymbosa* appear in a cluster at the tops of flower stalks. And individual flowers of

*M. abieticola,* also greenish, are branched on horizontal stems that separate them from the main stem.

**Elevation:** 5,200 to 9,200 feet
**Range:** Texas, New Mexico, Arizona, and northern Mexico

*M. abieticola*

*M. porphyrea*

*M. corymbosa*

# Sidebells, Wintergreen

## Orthilia secunda

**Wintergreen family (Pyrolaceae)**

A low evergreen perennial growing to about 8 inches tall, sidebells has dark shiny leaves and a flower stalk bearing whitish-green, bell-shaped blossoms all turned to one side. Individual flowers are only ¼ inch long, with 5 petals and 10 stamens. Fruits develop into spherical capsules. Sidebells prefers shady habitats in moist coniferous forests and is extremely

widespread, occurring from Alaska to the Southwest and eastern US, northern Mexico, Central America, and Eurasia. It is the only species in the genus *Orthilia* and was once included in the genus *Pyrola*. The wintergreen family has 4 genera and about 40 species.

**Elevation:** 7,000 to 9,500 feet
**Range:** widespread throughout North America, northern Mexico, Central America, and Eurasia

# Thurber's Bog Orchid

## Platanthera limosa

**Orchid family (Orchidaceae)**

Thurber's bog orchid can grow from 8 inches to 3 feet tall, with lance-shaped leaves scattered along the stem. Looking closely at the flower structure, one can see that the petals are yellow-green with a prominent yellow lip. The dorsal sepal forms a hood over the column, and a long spur protrudes at the base of each flower. This orchid prefers wet habitats in mixed conifer forests and often occurs along shady streams or in hillside seeps nestled among other vegetation. Widespread in Mexico, it reaches its northern limit in Arizona and New Mexico. Just to the north it is replaced by *P. purpurascens,* a species common in the Rocky Mountains that reaches its southern limit on Mount Graham in Arizona. *P. purpurascens* is easily distinguished from *P. limosa* by the much shorter spurs on the flowers.

**Elevation:** 6,300 to 9,150 feet
**Range:** New Mexico, southern Arizona, and Mexico

# Stonecrop

## Sedum stelliforme

**Crassula family (Crassulaceae)**

A low-growing, somewhat inconspicuous perennial with succulent leaves and stems, stonecrop grows to a height of only about 8 inches and is often seen nestled in rock crevices. White clusters of ½-inch-long blossoms occur on the stem tips. Each flower has 5 petals and 5 sepals and is followed by 5 erect capsules that split open lengthwise as they dry and mature. Leaves are lance-shaped and almost cylindrical; roots are creeping rhizomes. Flowers of *Sedum* species range from white to pink, yellow, or red. Herbalists use the mucilaginous juice of the mashed leaves as a soothing treatment for minor wounds, burns, insect bites, and skin irritations.

**Elevation:** 7,000 to 9,500 feet
**Range:** Arizona, New Mexico, and northern Mexico

# False Solomon Seal

## Smilacina racemosa

**Lily family (Liliaceae)**

*S. stellata*

A perennial growing to 3 feet tall from creeping rhizomes, false Solomon seal's stems emerge in early spring and produce alternating lance-shaped leaves in distinct rows. Note the prominent parallel venation on the leaves. Tiny white blossoms are borne in dense clusters at the stem tips. Fruits consist of ¼-inch red berries, often dotted with purple. Only 2 species of *Smilacina* occur in the West and can be easily distinguished. Starflower, *S. stellata,* is a smaller plant overall, reaching only 2 feet in height and bearing few flowers on loosely branched stalks. Berries are reddish-purple turning to black. Both species are found in moist, shady coniferous forests, along stream banks, and in meadows. Root and leaf preparations of false Solomon seal have been used by herbalists to treat sore throats and colds, and as poultices for swellings, boils, and wounds.

**Elevation:** 6,000 to 10,000 feet
**Range:** widespread throughout North America

# Hooded Ladies' Tresses

## Spiranthes romansoffiana

**Orchid family (Orchidaceae)**

Hooded ladies' tresses bears delicate white flowers arranged in vertical rows that spiral around slender stalks. Plants can range from 6 to 18 inches in height, depending on geographic location and environmental conditions, and they can be difficult to find among dense grasses and sedges in mountain meadows where they occur. The flowers are fragrant, white, and tubular, with the sepals and petals forming a hood over the downward-curving lip. Pollination studies have shown that bees are the primary pollinators. Shiny, lance-shaped succulent leaves are found only at the base of the plant. Hooded ladies' tresses blooms in late summer, is found in wet meadows, bogs, and along streams, and is widely distributed in the West. The related *S. delitescens* is a rare southern Arizona endemic, and *S. magnicamporum* is widespread in the Great Plains, reaching its southern limit in Bernalillo County, New Mexico.

**Elevation:** 8,500 to 9,500 feet
**Range:** widespread throughout much of North America

# Deers Ears, Monument Plant

Swertia radiata

**Gentian family (Gentianaceae)**

A biennial that begins as a basal rosette of leaves in the first year, deers ears shoots up a tall—up to 7 feet—flower stalk in its second year, given adequate soil moisture. Clusters of greenish flowers emerge from the leaf axils along the upper portion of the stout stems. Individual blossoms have purple spots and streaks and unusual fringed nectar glands on each of the 4 petals. Leaves are whorled on the stems, and basal leaves resemble the shape of deer's ears, giving the plant its common name. Deers ears is found in mountain meadows and open forests throughout the West and is considered good browse for deer and elk. A tea of the leaves was used by Native Americans to rub on the bodies of hunters and their horses to give them strength. The related star gentian, *S. perennis,* is a smaller plant with blue flowers that occurs from Canada to New Mexico.

**Elevation:** 5,000 to 10,000 feet
**Range:** Washington to Mexico

# Corn Lily, False Hellebore

## Veratrum californicum

**Lily family (Liliaceae)**

The stout leafy stems of corn lily stand 4 to 8 feet tall, topped by branched flower stalks densely covered with creamy-white blossoms in the height of the flowering season. Looking closely at the flowers, one can see a V-shaped greenish gland at the base of each of the 6 petal-like segments. After the plant flowers, 1-inch-long fruits develop, containing yellowish winged seeds. Broad, pleated leaves clasp the central stems and can reach up to a foot in length. Corn lily grows in riparian habitats and moist meadows throughout the West and can be extremely poisonous to livestock. The related *V. viride,* also poisonous, has been used in dilute concentrations as a remedy for sore throat, bronchitis, pneumonia, fever, and heart disorders. It is used today in pharmaceutical drugs to slow the heartbeat and lower blood pressure. The powdered root is used as an insecticide.

**Elevation:** 7,500 to 9,500 feet
**Range**: widespread throughout the western US

# Canada Violet

## Viola canadensis

**Violet family (Violaceae)**

Canada violet is a perennial herb easily recognized by its resemblance to the familiar cultivated violets. White, 1-inch-wide flowers appear in the upper leaf axils, and typically a spot of yellow is visible at the base of each petal, along with delicate purple lines that serve as nectar guides for pollinators. All petals are tinged with purple on the back. The classic heart-shaped leaves have pointed tips, are finely toothed, and range from 1 to 3 inches in length. Canada violet can grow to 12 inches in height but is usually much shorter, forming small clumps in moist, shady habitats. The leaves have been used medicinally as a diuretic, laxative, and expectorant. Native Americans used the roots to induce vomiting in cases of poisoning.

**Elevation:** 6,000 to 11,500 feet
**Range:** widespread throughout much of North America

# Golden Columbine

## Aquilegia chrysantha

**Buttercup family (Ranunculaceae)**

A large and showy multiple-stemmed perennial, golden columbine prefers rich, moist soils and can grow to 4 feet in height under favorable conditions. Three-inch-wide, golden yellow flowers face upward with 5 rounded funnel-shaped petals and 5 long spurs. A cluster of stamens protrudes from the center of each bloom. Bluish-green basal leaves divide into leaflets with scalloped, rounded lobes. At least 8 species of columbine occur in the West, with golden columbine the most common in Arizona and New Mexico. Red columbine, *A.desertorum,* less common in the Southwest, has smaller, downward-facing red and yellow blossoms. Reaching its southern limit in northern Arizona and New Mexico is the handsome blue columbine, *A.coerula,* the state flower of Colorado. Columbines are highly desirable for use in gardens, and many attractive hybrids and cultivars have been developed by the nursery industry.

**Elevation:** 3,000 to 11,000 feet
**Range:** Colorado to New Mexico, Arizona, and northern Mexico

*A.desertorum*

# Ragleaf Bahia

## Bahia dissecta

**Sunflower family (Asteraceae)**

Ragleaf bahia is an upright perennial growing to about 2 feet in height. Flower heads are flat with bright yellow rays and darker yellow disk flowers. Compound, highly dissected leaves are widely spaced on the stems. Ragleaf bahia is found in grasslands, pinyon juniper woodland, and pine forests. Navajos used the plant as a treatment for menstrual pain and arthritis, and Zunis used it for headaches and rheumatism. The related, desert-adapted Bahia, *B. absinthifolia,* is a low-growing perennial with gray foliage typically divided into three lobes. It occurs in open desert, rocky canyons, and grasslands from 2,300 to 5,500 feet.

**Elevation:** 5,000 to 9,000 feet
**Range:** Wyoming to Arizona and northern Mexico

# Golden Draba

## Draba aurea

**Mustard family (Brassicaceae)**

Growing to only about 8 inches in height, this small but showy mustard grows in clumps and bears golden yellow flowers in clusters on the stem tips. Each bloom has 4 petals, 4 hairy sepals, and 6 stamens. The long, flat seedpods can be either straight or twisted into a corkscrew shape. Basal leaves are finely hairy, about 2 inches long, and arranged in a rosette. Golden draba is abundant in pine and mixed conifer forests and in alpine zones. *D. petrophila,* found mainly in rock crevices, is similar in appearance and occurs only in southern Arizona and northern Sonora. A decoction of the leaves of *D. helleriana* was used by Navajos to treat serious coughs and gonorrhea. There are about 300 species in the genus *Draba,* all having yellow or white flowers.

**Elevation:** 5,000 to 12,000 feet
**Range:** widely distributed in western North America

# Western Sneezeweed

## Dugaldia hoopesii

**Aster family (Asteraceae)**

Western sneezeweed is a common meadow and roadside plant throughout the West and often grows in large, dense patches, with individual plants reaching 2 to 4 feet in height. The 3-inch-wide, yellow to orange-yellow sunflower-like heads are laden with flowers that attract a variety of insect and butterfly pollinators. Narrow leaves at the base of the plant grow up to a foot in length, with woolly hairs and toothless margins. Pollen from the flowers reputedly can cause an allergic reaction, including sneezing, in some individuals. Navajos have used the roots as a chewing gum and boiled the flowers with juniper ash to make a yellow dye.

**Elevation:** 7,000 to 11,000 feet
**Range:** Wyoming and Oregon to California, Arizona, and New Mexico

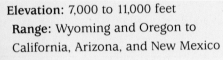

# Torrey's Crag Lily

## Echeandia flavescens

**Lily family (Liliaceae)**

Torrey's crag lily bears amber-colored blooms on a slender leafless stalk. The 1-inch-wide flower forms a flattened star shape with 6 petal-like segments, each with a prominent green or brown midvein. The narrow and grasslike leaves feature parallel veins and are found only at the base of the plant. After flowering, the fruits develop into oblong capsules that dry and split at maturity, releasing the seeds. Torrey's crag lily is found from grassland to mixed conifer forests, often in open, rocky sites. Chandler's crag lily, *E. chandleri,* has wider leaves with cross-veins and occurs in southern coastal parts of Texas and the lower Rio Grande Valley.

**Elevation:** 6,000 to 9,000 feet
**Range:** Arizona, New Mexico, Texas, and northern Mexico

# Golden Eye

## Heliomeris multiflora

**Sunflower family (Asteraceae)**

Golden eye is a perennial herb growing up to 3 feet in height and branching profusely from the base. In a good year it produces a mass of golden yellow flowers. Flower heads are about 2 inches wide, with darker yellow disk flowers that become rounded or conical in shape as the flowers fade. The lance-shaped leaves oppose each other along the stems and have a rough, "sandpaper" texture. Golden eye is found in a variety of habitats including open hillsides, clearings, meadows, and roadsides. In Southwest mountains, golden eye could be mistaken for ox eye, *Heliopsis parviflora*. Ox eye bears similar golden-yellow flower heads but has triangular and toothed leaves.
It has a narrower distribution, occurring only in southeastern Arizona to southwestern Texas and northern Mexico.

**Elevation:** 4,500 to 9,500 feet
**Range**: Montana to New Mexico, Arizona, Nevada, and California

# Common Alumroot

## Heuchera parvifolia

**Saxifrage family (Saxifragaceae)**

A perennial to 2 feet in height, common alumroot has slender, reddish flowering stems that arise from a basal rosette of leaves. Tiny, pale yellow flowers are clustered in small spikes along the stems. The sepals are yellowish and broad; actual petals are small and white. Leaves of common alumroot are rounded in shape, with several hairy, toothed lobes cut along the leaf margins. It is typically found on cliffs, gravelly hillsides, and rocky slopes. Dried and powdered leaves and roots of alumroot were used by Native Americans in the Northwest as a digestive aid and externally to treat sores, cuts, bites, rashes, ulcers, and wounds. Modern herbalists recognize the powerful astringent properties of these plants and use preparations of leaves and roots to stop minor bleeding and reduce inflammation.

**Elevation:** 7,000 to 11,500 feet
**Range:** widely distributed in western North America

# St. John's Wort

## Hypericum formosum

**St. John's Wort family (Gutiferae)**

A perennial herb from creeping rootstocks, St. John's wort can grow to 2 feet in height, with golden yellow blossoms on branched stem tips. The flowers have 4 or 5 petals and numerous stamens. Oval leaves occur in pairs along the stems. Both leaves and flowers are covered with tiny black dots or glands containing hypericin, a medicinally active compound that makes a red stain on the skin. St. John's wort thrives in open moist meadows throughout the West. A related species, *H. perforatum,* is a European introduction that has naturalized in much of eastern and northwestern North America. It is used externally in treatments for sprains, swellings, and wounds. Internally it has been taken for anxiety, insomnia, and mild depression. Modern research supports its effectiveness as a treatment for mild depression. The use of this plant internally or externally can cause burns on the skin in some individuals when exposed to sunlight.

**Elevation:** 5,000 to 9,000 feet
**Range:** Wyoming to Arizona, southern California, and Mexico

# Mountain Gromwell, Puccoon

## Lithospermum cobrense

**Borage family (Boraginaceae)**

Yellow, funnel-shaped flowers on upright, coiled stems characterize mountain gromwell. Funnel-shaped corollas flare at the throat with five petal lobes. Leaves are lance-shaped, and stems and leaves are covered with short stiff hairs (a characteristic of many members of the Borage family). The genus name *Lithospermum* means "stone seed" and refers to the hard, white, shiny seeds or nutlets produced by the plants. Puccoon, a common name for the genus, is an Algonquian word for plants used as dyes. Several species produce a purple dye, though *L. cobrense* does not. Mountain gromwell produces a second set of inconspicuous late-season blooms that remain closed, self-pollinate, and produce the bulk of the seeds for the year. The much more common fringed gromwell, *L. incisum,* with fringed corolla lobes, also occurs in the Southwest. It is found from Canada to Arizona, New Mexico, and Texas.

**Elevation:** 5,000 to 9,000 feet
**Range:** Texas, New Mexico, Arizona, and Mexico

# Yellow Monkey Flower

## Mimulus guttatus

**Figwort family (Scrophulariaceae)**

Highly variable in terms of size, yellow monkey flower can occur as a single-stemmed plant just a few inches high or a multi-branched shrub up to 3 feet tall. The bright lemon-yellow, snapdragon-like corollas bear characteristic reddish spots on the lower lobes that serve as guides for bee pollinators. Leaves are dark green, oval to round, opposed, and toothed. Yellow monkey flower has hollow stems, can be annual or perennial depending on conditions, and is found along streams, seeps, and other wet places. With ample moisture it can thrive in a variety of habitats throughout a broad elevational and geographic range. The Shoshoni traditionally made a poultice of the leaves for burns, cuts, and wounds. Other Native Americans ate the leaves raw or cooked, as a vegetable. Crimson monkey flower, *Mimulus cardinalis,* has rich red, tubular corollas, is pollinated by hummingbirds, and occurs in shady, streamside environments from 2,000 to 8,500 feet.

**Elevation:** 500 to 9,500 feet
**Range:** Alaska to northern Mexico

*M. cardinalis*

*M. cardinalis*

# Hooker Evening Primrose

## Oenothera elata ssp. hookeri

**Evening Primrose family (Onagraceae)**

A showy biennial, hooker evening primrose is notable for its height, up to 4 feet under good conditions. Three-inch-wide, bright yellow flowers fading to orange emerge from leaf axils along the single erect stem. Each blossom bears 4 petals, 4 reflexed sepals, 8 stamens, and a cross-shaped stigma. The flowers are followed by slender upright pods that dry and split at maturity, spilling out tiny seeds. Leaves are lance-shaped with wavy margins and can be up to 9 inches in length at the base of the plant. Hooker evening primrose occurs in a variety of habitats from grassland to coniferous forests. The Navajo and Zuni used the plant in treatments for sores and swellings.

**Elevation:** 3,500 to 9,500 feet
**Range:** Washington to Baja California, southern Colorado to Texas and Sonora, Mexico

# Parry Lousewort

## Pedicularis parryi

**Figwort family (Scrophulariaceae)**

Growing to a height of about 1½ feet, parry lousewort is a common meadow plant in the subalpine and alpine zones. Creamy-white to yellowish flowers occur on a tall spike interspersed with green leafy bracts. Blossoms have an arched upper lip that resembles a bird's head, and a broader lower lip curves downward. The mainly basal lower leaves are fernlike, long and narrow, deeply divided, and toothed. A well-known related species known as elephant head, *P. groenlandica,* has a pink corolla with an elongated upper lip that forms what resembles an upturned elephant's trunk. It occurs throughout much of northern and western North America. The name lousewort refers to the use of *Pedicularis* species to rid animals of lice. These plants have also been used as a poultice for cuts, sores, and swellings.

**Elevation:** 7,500 to 12,000 feet
**Range:** Wyoming and Montana south to New Mexico and Arizona

# Mountain Parsley

## Pseudocymopterus montanus

**Parsley family (Apiaceae)**

Mountain parsley is an herbaceous perennial with a long, slender taproot. Flowers consist of tiny blossoms grouped together in flat-topped clusters and varying from bright yellow to orange or maroon in color. After the plant flowers, tiny winged fruits develop. Plants grow from 8 inches to 2 feet in height with fernlike, pinnately divided leaves. Vegetative characteristics of the plant vary greatly throughout the range of the species. Mountain parsley is found in pine and mixed conifer forests, in meadows, on rocky slopes, and in grasslands. The genus name, *Pseudocymopterus,* refers to its similarity to *Cymopterus,* another genus in the parsley family.

**Elevation:** 5,500 to 12,000 feet
**Range:** Wyoming to Utah, south
to Mexico

# Pinedrops

## Pterospora andromeda

**Heather family (Ericaceae)**

A slender, unbranched, reddish to purplish, sticky plant, pinedrops produces creamy-white to pale yellow, bell-shaped flowers that hang downward on elongated spikes. Small round fruits dry and split open as they mature, releasing many winged seeds. Leaves are merely scale-like, translucent bracts along the lower stems. The stems grow for only one season, but dried stalks remain standing for years. Pinedrops is a saprophyte—that is, it lacks chlorophyll and obtains nutrients from decaying organic matter in the soil. Indian pipe, *Monotropa latisquama,* is a similar plant with fewer flowers that have distinctly separate petals. The petals of pinedrops flowers are united into a single corolla.

**Elevation:** 6,000 to 9,500 feet
**Range:** throughout western North America and northeastern US

# Cutleaf Coneflower, Brown-Eyed Susan

## Rudbeckia laciniata

**Sunflower family (Asteraceae)**

Cutleaf coneflower is a lush perennial with large leaves and flower heads. Leaves are deeply divided, pointed, toothed, and up to 8 inches in length. Entire plants can grow to 7 feet tall under ideal conditions. The 5-inch-wide flower heads have drooping rays and a cone-shaped mass of greenish-yellow disk flowers. Cutleaf coneflower prefers moist habitats and rich soils in wet meadows and along mountain streams. The related black-eyed Susan, *Rudbeckia hirta,* is a smaller plant with rough, hairy stems, undivided leaves, and a central cone of dark, purplish disk flowers. This eastern species has spread through parts of Canada to Colorado.

**Elevation:** 5,000 to 8,500 feet
**Range:** Canada to Arizona, New Mexico, Texas, and southeastern US

# Nodding Groundsel

## Senecio bigelovii

**Sunflower family (Asteraceae)**

Nodding groundsel is aptly named, as the flower heads dangle in a downward-facing manner from stout leafy stems. Unlike many *Senecio* species, this one lacks ray flowers. Heads consist of dense ½-inch-wide bundles of yellowish disk flowers. The bracts beneath

the flowers are arranged side by side, not overlapping, and they are more or less the same length. Flowers are followed by one-seeded fruits called achenes, characterisic of the sunflower family. Nodding groundsel can grow 1 to 3 feet in height and has alternate, toothed, lance-shaped leaves. It is restricted to moist grassy slopes and coniferous forests at or above 7,000 feet. *Senecio* comprises an exceptionally large genus, with about 3,000 species worldwide. Many Western species are extremely poisonous to cattle and horses. The name *Senecio* means "old man" and refers to the whisker-like bristles attached to the fruits.

**Elevation:** 7,000 to 11,000 feet
**Range:** western Colorado to Arizona and New Mexico

# Goldenrod

## Solidago wrightii

**Sunflower family (Asteraceae)**

Goldenrod is an herbaceous perennial that creates a showy display in the late summer and fall with its golden yellow flowers clustered on long spikes. Flower heads consist of ray and disk flowers, though the rays are small and inconspicuous. Leaves are alternating and considerably larger at the base of the plant. *S. wrightii* is found in rocky canyons, grasslands, oak woodland, and conifer forests. Although this species is restricted to the Southwest, the genus is widespread and well-represented throughout much of North America. The genus name *Solidago* is from the Latin *solidus* (whole) and *ago* (to make)—to make whole or cure—referring to the curative powers of the plant. A tea of the

leaves has long been used to relieve intestinal gas and cramps and as a cold remedy and a tonic for the kidneys. The related Canada goldenrod, *Solidago canadensis,* contains the compound quercitin, used to treat inflammation and bleeding of the kidneys. Goldenrod was once called "woundwort" due to its effectiveness in stopping the blood flow from wounds.

**Elevation:** 3,500 to 9,500 feet
**Range:** western Texas to Arizona

# Woolly Mullein, Flannel Mullein

## Verbascum thapsus

**Figwort family (Scrophulariaceae)**

An introduced European weed that has naturalized throughout much of North America, woolly mullein is an unmistakable biennial with dense, velvety hairs on the leaves and a stout, erect flower spike packed with 1-inch-wide lemon-yellow flowers. In the first year the plant forms a rosette of leaves. The ensuing flower stalk in year two can grow from 1 to 8 feet in height depending on conditions. Woolly mullein has long been used in Europe and the US as a remedy for a variety of respiratory ailments including colds, coughs, asthma, sore throat, and bronchitis. The leaves are often smoked to relieve congestion. Woolly mullein has also been poulticed as a treatment for sprains, swelling, wounds, and inflammation, and oil from the flowers has been used as an earache remedy. It prefers open habitats including meadows, fields, disturbed sites, and roadsides. In some states it has spread so aggressively it has been listed as a noxious weed.

**Elevation:** 5,000 to 8,000 feet
**Range:** throughout North America

# Indian Paintbrush

## Castilleja patriotica

**Figwort family (Scrophulariaceae)**

Indian paintbrush is a wildflower that is common and easily recognized throughout the West. Various species occur from low deserts into the highest alpine zones. The showy parts of the flowers are actually colorful bracts surrounding the inconspicuous tubular corollas, which are partially hidden. *C. patriotica* has red-orange bracts and a pale yellow corolla tube with a long narrow upper lip and a short broad lower lip. Flowers produce ample nectar for hummingbirds that frequent the flowers. As is true of most paintbrushes, this species is a partial parasite on the roots of other plants. *C. patriotica* has a limited distribution in the Southwest, reaching its northern limit in southeastern Arizona. Wyoming paintbrush, *C. linariaefolia,* is similar and much more widespread, occurring from Wyoming to Arizona and New Mexico at elevations of 5,000 to 10,000 feet.

**Elevation:** 8,000 to 9,000 feet
**Range:** southeastern Arizona and northern Mexico

# Western Wallflower

## Erysimum capitatum

**Mustard family (Brassicaceae)**

A short-lived perennial growing to 3 feet in height, the handsome western wallflower is a widespread and variable species with showy flowers clustered around stem tips. The colorful, ¾-inch-wide, fragrant flowers vary in color from burnt orange to lemon yellow or maroon. Fruits develop into narrow upright pods that burst open to release the

tiny seeds. Leaves are grayish-green and lance-shaped with small teeth. Related European species are often seen growing against walls, hence the name of wallflower. Western wallflower occurs in a broad elevational range and a variety of habitats from grassland to mixed conifer forest. At the lower elevations the flowers tend to be yellow, and in higher country, orange or maroon. Powdered pods of western wallflower were used by Navajos as a snuff for cases of nasal congestion, and Hopis have used the plant as a treatment for tuberculosis. The whole plant was used ceremonially by the Zuni to help bring forth rains.

**Elevation:** 2,500 to 9,500 feet

**Range:** Canada to California, Arizona, and New Mexico

# Coral Bells

## Heuchera sanguinea

### Saxifrage family (Saxifragaceae)

D ainty, bell-shaped, deep pink to coral-red flower clusters hang on leafless stalks above the basal leaves of coral bells. The dark green, rounded leaves have pointed lobes and grow in a low, loose rosette. Coral bells is often seen in shaded rocky canyons and slopes in oak woodland, and in conifer forests. Although it has a limited distribution in the Southwest, coral bells is widely grown as an ornamental. Related species of *Heuchera* are known as alum-root and have yellow or pale pink blossoms.

**Elevation:** 4,000 to 8,500 feet

**Range:** southern Arizona, southwestern New Mexico, and northern Mexico

# Skyrocket, Scarlet Gilia

## Ipomopsis aggregata

**Phlox family (Polemoniaceae)**

Skyrocket is an attractive perennial that superficially resembles a penstemon but is actually a member of the phlox family. Brilliant red-orange, tubular blossoms emerge on one side of a stalk that reaches up to 3 feet in height. The flowers have flared and pointed petal lobes, cream-colored spots at the throat, and a 3-part stigma characteristic of the family. The sticky, foul-smelling leaves are pinnately divided into narrow, linear lobes. This common and showy wildflower is frequently cultivated in gardens throughout the West. Navajos used the plant as treatment for spider bites and stomach disease and for application on the bodies of hunters for good luck.

**Elevation:** 5,000 to 9,000 feet
**Range:** Canada to California, Arizona, New Mexico, and northern Mexico

# Beardtongue

## Penstemon barbatus

**Figwort family (Scrophulariaceae)**

The scarlet, tubular corollas of beardtongue dangle along one side of the 1- to 3-foot-tall flowering stems. White spots are often visible on the lower corolla lobes that are reflexed back. The upper lip projects forward. Leaves are long, narrow, and undivided and form a basal rosette in the first year. Given ample moisture, multiple flower stalks will arise in the second season. Beardtongue is pollinated by hummingbirds and is often planted in gardens to attract these colorful birds. The common name of beardtongue refers to the sterile, brushy stamen that can be seen in the corollas of this and other members of the genus *Penstemon*.

**Elevation:** 4,000 to 10,000 feet
**Range:** southern Colorado to Arizona, New Mexico, Texas, and northern Mexico

# Pine-leaf Penstemon

Penstemon pinnifolius

**Figwort family (Scrophulariaceae)**

Pine-leaf penstemon, unlike many members of the genus, forms a low mound and does not send up tall flower stalks. Instead, the orange-red, tubular blossoms rise just above the compact, needle-like foliage. Three lower petal lobes of the corolla are distinct and spreading; the 2 upper lobes project upward. The flowers are highly attractive to hummingbirds throughout the late-summer blooming season. After flowering, rounded upright pods with pointed tips will develop, splitting at maturity to release the seeds. Although several *Penstemon* species occur in Southwest mountains, pine-leaf penstemon is so distinct it is not likely to be mistaken for any other except the rare *P. discolor.* Pine-leaf penstemon has a limited distribution in the Southwest, reaching its northern limit in southeastern Arizona and southwestern New Mexico.

**Elevation:** 5,000 to 8,500 feet
**Range:** southeastern Arizona, southwestern New Mexico, and northern Mexico

# Thurber Cinquefoil

## Potentilla thurberi

**Rose family (Rosaceae)**

The rich maroon color of Thurber cinquefoil blossoms is unique among mountain wildflowers. Individual blooms are bowl-shaped, with 5 petals and many stamens in the center. Leaves are toothed and palmate with 5 leaflets, as is typical of the *Potentilla* genus. The word cinquefoil derives from the French word for "5 leaves." Thurber cinquefoil plants can grow to 3 feet in height, bearing small clusters of flowers on the stem tips. It is typically found in pine and mixed conifer forests and is limited in distribution to the southwestern US and northern Mexico. The related *P. hippeana* blooms yellow, is widespread throughout western North America, and generally occurs in open grassy meadows. It has been used by the Navajo to treat burns, sores, and injuries.

**Elevation:** 5,000 to 8,000 feet
**Range:** Arizona, New Mexico, and northern Mexico

# Mexican Campion

## Silene laciniata

**Pink family (Caryophyllaceae)**

Mexican campion is one of the most handsome of the campions, or members of the genus *Silene*. Flowers are brilliant red and large—about 1½ inches wide. Each petal is deeply cut into 4 sections with sharp points, giving the flower a fringed, ornate appearance. Leaves are sticky and lance-shaped; plants can grow to 3 feet but are often much smaller. Mexican campion is encountered in shady or open sites

in pine and mixed conifer forests. The related *S. scouleri* is found at similar elevations, blooms pale pink, has a striped, balloon-like calyx, and occurs from Canada to Mexico.

**Elevation:** 5,500 to 9,000 feet
**Range:** California to west Texas and northern Mexico

# Nodding Onion

## Allium cernuum

**Lily family (Liliaceae)**

Nodding onion is a perennial herb bearing a hanging cluster of pink flowers at the tips of slender leafless stalks. Flowers are bell-shaped, have 6 rounded petals and long stamens, and can range in color from pale pink to white to deep rose. The basal leaves are grasslike and smell strongly of onion. Nodding onion is edible, and the leaves and bulbs were widely eaten by Native Americans and early settlers. It was consumed either raw or cooked, as both a food and flavoring, and was often dried for winter use. This and other *Allium* species have also been used as medicine for treating cuts, burns, bites, and stings, as well as colds and sore throats. Also common and widespread is Geyer's onion, *A. geyeri,* with deep pink flowers in an erect cluster and netted, fibrous bulb coats. It occurs at elevations of 5,000 to 10,000 feet, from Wyoming and Colorado to Arizona and New Mexico. Be aware that when not in flower, wild onions resemble mountain death camas, *Zigadenus* species, which are highly poisonous—always make certain of the identity of a plant before tasting it.

**Elevation:** 5,000 to 8,500 feet
**Range:** throughout temperate North America

# Fireweed

## Chamerion angustifolium

**Evening primrose family (Onagraceae)**

Often growing in dazzling large patches after fires, fireweed—a 2- to 7-foot-tall herbaceous perennial—spreads easily from underground stems. Numerous flowers emerge on each of several long terminal spikes. The 4-petaled flower has 8 stamens and a cross-shaped stigma. Flowers lowest on the stalk bloom first, then produce slender upright pods. As they mature, these pods split to release tiny seeds, each with silky hairs that facilitate dispersal by the wind. Veins of the leaves of fireweed join together within the leaf margin, forming a noticeable inner border. Leaves turn scarlet red in the fall of the year.

**Elevation:** 7,000 to 11,500 feet
**Range:** throughout much of North America

# Wheeler Thistle

## Cirsium wheeleri

**Aster family (Asteraceae)**

A perennial with prickly foliage and striking rose-purple flowers, Wheeler thistle can grow up to 4 feet in height. Tubular disk flowers are packed tightly together in a 1½-inch-wide head and provide ample nectar for a host of butterfly and insect pollinators. Lance-shaped leaves alternate on the stems and are deeply lobed, with spiny teeth along the margins. Many thistles are actually European natives that have spread aggressively and become serious pests in parts of North America. Western tribes have used the stems and roots of thistles as a vegetable and consumed it either raw or cooked. Navajos used the plants to treat chills, fever, and eye diseases.

**Elevation:** 5,000 to 9,000 feet
**Range:** southern Arizona and New Mexico

# Shooting Star

## Dodecatheon pulchellum

**Primrose family (Primulaceae)**

Four or 5 rosy-pink petals sweep back from the downward-pointing tips of shooting star blossoms. A yellow collar is visible at the base of the petals, and the stamens unite to form the point. Flower stalks rise

up to 2 feet from a clump of broad, lance-shaped leaves. Shooting stars are "buzz pollinated"—that is, the fine pollen is released onto bees as they cling to the flowers and rapidly vibrate their wings. After flowering, fruits mature into upright capsules that split open lengthwise to release the seeds. These attractive, unusual flowers are seen in moist mountain meadows and along stream banks.

**Elevation:** 6,500 to 9,500 feet
**Range:** Alaska to Mexico

# Wild Geranium

## Geranium caespitosum

### Geranium family (Geraniaceae)

The reddish-pink flowers of wild geranium make a common and lovely sight along shaded forest trails. A close look at the blossoms shows whitish streaks and hairs on the petals, not seen on related species. Plants grow to 1½ feet tall with profusely branching stems. Leaves are deeply palmately lobed and cut, and soft hairs can be observed on both leaf surfaces. An equally common, related species, *G.richardsonii,* has smaller flowers that are white with purple veins. Geraniums have long been used as a folk remedy for sore throat, gum disease, ulcers, nosebleeds, and rashes. The entire genus is often called cranesbill in reference to the long pointed fruits that resemble a bird's beak.

**Elevation:** 5,000 to 9,000 feet
**Range:** Colorado and Utah to Mexico

# Lemmon's Sage, Lemmon's Salvia

## Salvia lemmoni

**Mint family (Lamiaceae)**

Although Lemmon's sage has a limited distribution in the Southwest, it adds much color to the landscape where it occurs. A multiple-stemmed perennial, somewhat woody at the base, it produces a profusion of deep rose-pink flowers in the late summer. The tubular blossoms are hummingbird pollinated, and any large patch of *S. lemmoni* makes a good place to observe hummingbird activity. Corollas have long upper lips that project forward and lower lips that bend downward. Plants grow 1 to 2 feet in height and bear aromatic, oval-shaped leaves. We find many species of *Salvia* in the western US, and this one bears a resemblance to *S. microphylla,* a popular landscape plant from Chihuahua, Mexico. Some Native Americans of the Southwest burn the leaves and stems of white sage, *S. apiana,* in ceremonies. The common name of sage is also used in reference to members of the genus *Artemesia*—for example, sagebrush, *A. tridentata.*

**Elevation:** 6,000 to 8,000 feet
**Range:** southern Arizona and northern Mexico

# Glossary

*Achene*  a small, hard, one-seeded fruit

*Alkaloid*  a toxic substance produced in a plant, often possessing medicinal properties

*Annual*  a plant with a life cycle completed in one year

*Anther*  the enlarged, pollen-containing part of a stamen

*Axil*  area in the angle formed by the upper side of the leaf where it joins the stem

*Banner*  upper petal of a legume flower

*Basal*  at the base of the plant

*Biennial*  a plant with a life cycle completed in two years

*Bract*  a modified leaf, often at the base of a flower or flower cluster

*Bulb*  a thick, fleshy structure that forms below ground and functions in food storage

*Calyx*  collective term for the sepals of a flower, usually green

*Capsule*  a dry fruit with one or more compartments

*Corolla*  a collective term for a the petals of a flower, which may be independent or united

*Disk flower*  the small, tubular flowers present in the central part of a floral head, as in most members of the sunflower family

*Fruit*  the ripened ovary with its seed(s)

*Gland*  a small structure usually secreting oil or nectar

*Parasite*  a plant growing on and deriving nourishment from another living plant

*Pendulous*  hanging or drooping

*Perennial*  a plant with a life cycle of more than two years

*Petal*  a basic unit of the corolla, usually brightly colored

*Pinnate leaf*  leaflets arranged in two rows along a common axis

*Pistil*  the female part of the flower, including ovary, style, and stigma

*Pollen*  spores formed in the anthers that produce the male cells

*Pollination*  the transfer of pollen from an anther to a stigma

*Prostrate*  flat on the ground

*Ray flower*  a strap-like corolla present in many plants of the sunflower family

*Sepal*  one of the segments of the outer whorl of flower parts, usually green

*Stamen*  the male part of the flower, consisting of filament and anther

*Stigma*  the pollen-receptive part of a pistil

*Style*  the portion of the pistil between the ovary and the stigma

*Umbel*  a flower cluster in which all the flower stalks grow from the same point

# Additional Reading

Brown, David E., ed. *Biotic Communities of the Southwestern United States and Northwestern Mexico.* University of Utah Press, 1994.

Coleman, Ron. *The Wild Orchids of Arizona and New Mexico.* Cornell University Press, 2002.

Epple, Anne. *A Field Guide to the Plants of Arizona.* Falcon Publishing, Inc., 1995.

Foster, Steven, and Christopher Hobbs. *Western Medicinal Plants and Herbs.* Houghton Mifflin Company, 2002.

Kearney, Thomas, and Robert Peebles. *Arizona Flora.* University of California Press, 1960.

Kershaw, Linda. *Edible and Medicinal Plants of the West.* Lone Pine Publishing, 2000.

Kershaw, Linda, Andy MacKinnon, and Jim Pojar. *Plants of the Rocky Mountains.* Lone Pine Publishing, 1998.

Lehr, Harry J. *A Catalogue of the Flora of Arizona.* Desert Botanical Garden, 1978.

Moerman, Daniel. *Native American Ethnobotany.* Timber Press, 1998.

Niehaus, Theodore. *A Field Guide to Southwestern and Texas Wildflowers.* Houghton Mifflin Company, 1984.

Robertson, Leigh. *Southern Rocky Mountain Wildflowers.* Falcon Publishing, Inc.,1999.

Spellenberg, Richard. *National Audubon Society Field Guide to Wildflowers, Western Region.* Chanticleer Press, Inc., 2001.

Tilford, Gregory. *Edible and Medicinal Plants of the West.* Mountain Press Publishing Company, 1997.

# Index